From Childhood You Have Known

Guiding Children to Understand and Treasure the Bible

by Jill Nelson

Truth:78

From Childhood You Have Known—Guiding Children to Understand and Treasure the Bible

by Jill Nelson

Our vision at Truth78 is that the next generations know, honor, and treasure God, setting their hope in Christ alone, so that they will live as faithful disciples for the glory of God. Our mission is to inspire and equip the church and the home for the comprehensive discipleship of the next generation.

We equip churches and parents by producing curricula for Sunday School, Midweek Bible, Intergenerational, Youth, and Backyard Bible Club settings; vision-casting and training resources (many available free on our website) for both the church and the home; materials and training to help parents in their role in discipling children; and the Fighter Verses™ Bible memory program to encourage the lifelong practice and love of Bible memory.

Copyright © 2022 Jill Nelson. Illustrations Truth78. All rights reserved. No part of this publication may be reproduced in any form without written permission from Truth78.

Published in the United States of America by Truth78.

Scripture quotations are from the Holy Bible, English Standard Version® (ESV®), copyright © 2001 by Crossway, a publishing ministry of Good News Publishers. ESV Text Edition: 2016. Used by permission. All rights reserved.

ISBN: 978-1-952783-52-4

Truth:78

Equipping the Next Generations to Know, Honor, and Treasure God

Truth78.org
info@Truth78.org
(877) 400-1414

It is the duty of the church of God to maintain, in fullest vigor, every agency intended for the religious education of the young; to them we must look for the church of the future, and as we sow towards them so shall we reap. Children are to be taught to magnify the Lord; they ought to be well informed as to his wonderful doings in ages past, and should be made to know "his strength and his wonderful works he hath done." The best education is education in the best things.[1]

—Charles Spurgeon

We are a people of the Book. We know God through the Book. We meet Christ in the Book. We see the cross in the Book. Our faith and love are kindled by the glorious truths of the Book. We have tasted the divine majesty of the Word and are persuaded that the Book is God's inspired and infallible written revelation. Therefore, what the Book teaches matters. Doctrine is important for worship and life and mission. Education for Exultation is education saturated by the Bible.[2]

—John Piper

The issue of earning a living is not nearly so important as whether the next generation has direct access to the meaning of the Word of God. We need an education that puts the highest premium under God on knowing the meaning of God's Book, and growing in the abilities that will unlock its riches for a lifetime. It would be better to starve for lack of food than to fail to grasp the meaning of the book of Romans. Lord, let us not fail the next generation![3]

—John Piper

---

1 Charles Haddon Spurgeon. *The Treasury of David.* (New York: Funk & Wagnalls, 1886), 433.
2 John Piper. "Building Our Lives on the Bible." March 5, 2000. desiringgod.org/messages/building-our-lives-on-the-bible
3 John Piper. "A Compelling Reason for Rigorous Training of the Mind: Thoughts on the Significance of Reading." July 13, 2005. desiringgod.org/articles/a-compelling-reason-for-rigorous-training-of-the-mind

Table of Contents

Preface..7

Part 1
10 Priorities for Guiding Children to Understand and Treasure the Bible 8
   Introduction...8
   1. Impress upon children a reverence for the holy nature of the Bible..............10
   2. Demonstrate a genuine delight in God's Word...............................12
   3. Have a long-term strategy for acquainting children and youth with the entire Bible..13
   4. Emphasize the whole counsel of God.....................................15
   5. Teach children to rightly read and interpret Scripture by equipping them with age-appropriate Bible study skills.....................................18
   6. Guide and implore children to rightly respond to and apply God's Word..........20
   7. Instill in children the need for humble dependence on the Holy Spirit as they read and study the Bible...22
   8. Integrate and connect biblical truth to all of life............................23
   9. Foster a partnership that promotes biblical literacy in both home and church.....25
   10. Devote and prioritize the necessary time required to do points 1-9.............26
   Final Thoughts..27

Part 2
Equipping and Training Children to Read and Study the Bible............29
   Using this Section...29
   Reading and Studying the Bible: Preschool (Ages 3-4).........................32
   Reading and Studying the Bible: Kindergarten (Ages 5-6)......................35
   Reading and Studying the Bible: 1st-2nd Grade (Ages 7-8).....................38
   Reading and Studying the Bible: 3rd-5th Grade (Ages 9-11)....................43
   Reading and Studying the Bible: 6th-8th Grade (Ages 12-14)...................49

Appendix..55
   Key Verses Describing the Bible..56
   Bible and Memory Verse Activities.......................................57
      Books of the Bible Games...57
      Memory Verses..59
   Instructions for Sword Drills...61
   10 Essential Truths of the Gospel.......................................62
   About Truth78..64

Preface

"I'm starving Grandma. I'm starving!" These were the earnest and pleading words of my four-year-old grandson one day. He had just experienced a 24-hour stomach virus that had rendered him depleted of food. Now that he was finally feeling better, he became fully aware of the physical gnawing of his empty tummy. All he could think of was, "I need food! I want food!"

Jesus Himself can sympathize with that physical longing for life-sustaining food, but even more so. After all, how many of us have found ourselves out in the wilderness for 40 days without any food to eat? Starving! Furthermore, in that moment of extreme hunger, the devil came to tempt Jesus.

> ..."*If you are the Son of God, command these stones to become loaves of bread.*" ⁴*But he answered, "It is written,*
>
> "'*Man shall not live by bread alone, but by every word that comes from the mouth of God.*'" *(Matthew 4:3-4)*

What an amazing answer, packed with profound meaning regarding the Word of God! Do we sincerely believe this to be true about the Bible? Do we see God's Word as absolutely necessary for sustaining our lives? Do we long for it more than we hunger for food? Are we communicating this reality to our children? As we diligently provide children with the physical food they require, are we also setting the highest priority on providing them with the *spiritual food* that is needed for giving them an unshakable hope, fullness of joy, and life everlasting? In other words, are the children in our homes and churches being *fed* the Bible?

This booklet has been written to help inspire and better equip the church and home to raise up a generation of children who *know* and *love* the Bible. God has given us a Book like no other, and we have been given the great responsibility and privilege to pass its life-giving truth to the next generation. Their very life and eternal joy depend upon it!

Part 1
10 Priorities for Guiding Children to Understand and Treasure the Bible

Introduction

In Bible times, it was a traditional Jewish custom for parents to begin instructing their children in the Scriptures when they reached five years old (early childhood).[4] In the case of Timothy, we are told that his mother and grandmother were instrumental in that instruction (2 Timothy 1:5). At some point in Timothy's life, the Apostle Paul also became a teacher and mentor. In order to prepare and encourage Timothy to stand firm in his faith during the trials that were sure to come, Paul reminded Timothy,

> *But as for you, continue in what you have learned and have firmly believed, knowing from whom you learned it* [15]*and how from childhood you have been acquainted with the sacred writings, which are able to make you wise for salvation through faith in Christ Jesus.* [16]*All Scripture is breathed out by God and profitable for teaching, for reproof, for correction, and for training in righteousness,* [17]*that the man of God may be complete, equipped for every good work. (2 Timothy 3:14-17)*

These timeless words serve to remind every believer, in each successive generation, of the great responsibility entrusted to us. The sacred writings—only the Old Testament at that time—were diligently taught to Timothy in a manner that guided him toward

---
4 *The Reformation Study Bible*, edited by R. C. Sproul (Sanford, Fla.: Ligonier Ministries, 2005), 1764.

faith in Christ, trained him in godliness, and equipped him for a life of fruitful service.[5]

In other words, "acquainting" children with the Scriptures is not simply teaching them *facts about* the Bible. It's not simply making sure they read the Bible from Genesis to Revelation. It's not simply teaching them the essential doctrines of the Bible or encouraging them to memorize a certain number of verses. The aim and goal should be to...

> *...acquaint our children with the breadth, depth, and authority of Scripture so that they would come to know, honor, and treasure the God of the Bible, setting their hope in Christ alone, and be trained and equipped to live as His faithful disciples for the glory of God.*[6]

This statement could be used as a helpful definition of what is meant by "biblical literacy." Defined as such, biblical literacy aims toward *heart transformation*, resulting in repentance from sin, trusting in Christ alone for salvation, walking in newness of life, loving God as your greatest treasure, and submitting to His ways. In a sense, biblical literacy is the wood and fuel of Christian discipleship which, Lord willing, is set aflame by the Holy Spirit in the lives of our children and students. *We* cannot set the heart aflame (regeneration), but we are called to carefully instruct them in how to properly read, examine, study, meditate on, and rightly respond to the Bible, providing all the necessary wood and fuel for the Holy Spirit to act upon.

That said, is this what is actually happening in the majority of Christian homes and churches?

> *Every study of the internal life of the churches shows that they are becoming increasingly less literate biblically.*[7]

> *We will not believe more than we know, and we will not live higher than our beliefs. The many fronts of Christian compromise in this generation can be directly traced to biblical illiteracy in*

---

5 See also: John 20:31; Romans 10:17; Romans 15:4; John 17:17; Colossians 1:9-10; 2 Peter 1:3.
6 Adapted from the Truth78 Vision Statement: Truth78.org/vision-overview
7 David Wells. "The Soul-Shaping Reality of the Gospel: An Interview with David Wells." January 1, 2011. ligonier.org/learn/articles/soul-shaping-reality-gospel-interview-david-wells

> *the pews and the absence of biblical preaching and teaching in our homes and churches...This generation must get deadly serious about the problem of biblical illiteracy...* [8]

Unfortunately, when it comes to children and youth, I have seen the problem of biblical *illiteracy* creep into even the most biblically solid churches. There may be a wonderful variety of robust Bible classes for adults, and yet children's and youth classes might offer a minimal amount of actual Bible teaching. Furthermore, intentional and ongoing Bible instruction is often absent in many Christian homes. And finally, if we understand that biblical literacy is much more than an academic pursuit—not simply what they know about the Bible, but a pursuit that involves coming "to know, honor, and treasure the God of the Bible, setting their hope in Christ alone..."—then the manner in which we acquaint our children and youth with the Bible also must be considered.

So what would a serious commitment to biblical literacy look like in our homes and churches? What would serve to undergird and focus our efforts? I would like to propose 10 foundational priorities to consider.

1. Impress upon children a reverence for the holy nature of the Bible.

Years ago, I inherited a beautiful cut-glass beverage set that had been a wedding gift to my grandma. It is a valuable and precious heirloom. But what if you came to my house and saw that lovely beverage set filled with rusty nails, screws, nuts, and bolts in the garage? What would this communicate to you, and why would it matter?

Now consider the Bible. What will our children and students observe about our demeanor and interaction with God's Word? Will they observe reverence and honor? Will they see us handling and interacting with God's Word as if we hold a priceless treasure in our hands? Are we giving them an understanding of the magnitude of what it means that Scripture is *God-breathed*, meaning that God

---
[8] Albert Mohler. "The Scandal of Biblical Illiteracy: It's Our Problem." January 20, 2016. albertmohler.com/2016/01/20/the-scandal-of-biblical-illiteracy-its-our-problem-4

is the source and ultimate Author of the Bible and, therefore, the Bible holds absolute authority over our lives? Will they hear us speak in a manner that shows unwavering confidence in God's Word as absolute, unchanging Truth? (See these references on the *inerrancy* of Scripture: Proverbs 30:5; Isaiah 40:8; Isaiah 45:19; and John 17:17).[9] Will we demonstrate that the Bible is understandable, clearly telling us about the most important things, especially what is necessary for us to be saved and to live a life that is pleasing to God? (See these references on the *clarity* and *necessity* of Scripture: Psalm 119:130 and Romans 10:13-17.) Will we communicate to them that the Bible we hold in our hands is *complete* and contains everything that is needed for life and godliness? In other words, the Bible is *sufficient* to answer every spiritual question and need that we have (2 Timothy 3:15-17).

It used to be that most Bibles had very classic-looking covers with the words "The Holy Bible" front and center, "Holy" meaning set apart and utterly unique. However, many Bibles marketed for children today look more like comic books. Does that help or hinder children in having an awe-filled respect for God's Word?[10]

Both in the classroom and at home, our demeanor toward the Bible should reflect a holy reverence. On more than one occasion, I have stopped a Sunday school lesson because I observed children treating the Bible in a flippant or disrespectful manner: standing on their Bibles, using the Bible to sword fight with someone sitting next to them, throwing it haphazardly on the floor, or just playing with the pages. I reminded them that this is God's holy Word. It's not to be trifled with. One simple way to continually remind children of this is to say something like this: "Listen very carefully and pay attention. We are going to read from God's Word. God's words are holy, righteous, and good. They are the most special words of all!"

---

9 I highly recommend Jon Bloom's short article, "Be Ready to Answer Your Kids' Questions About the Bible," published on October 13, 2014, on desiringGod.org (desiringgod.org/articles/be-ready-to-answer-your-kids-questions-about-the-bible). Another resource that is extremely helpful for introducing children to the holy nature of the Bible is the book, *God's Word* by Sally Michael (Truth78.org/gods-word).

10 Also see "Four Compelling Reasons to Use a Printed Bible When Teaching," published August 22, 2019, at Truth78.org (Truth78.org/blog/post/four-reasons-to-use-a-printed-bible-when-teaching-children-and-youth-2).

2. Demonstrate a genuine delight in God's Word.

A while ago, I was reading a picture book to my grandchildren. As I was reading, I couldn't help but break out laughing. About midway through, I noticed my grandson wasn't looking at the book anymore, he was looking at me. When I turned to him, he smiled and said, "Grandma, I can tell that you really like this book! I like it, too." Guess what, the next time he came to my house, he went right for that book.

Our children notice when we genuinely delight in something. And when we delight in it, it is more likely that they will be drawn to it, too. Look at these verses from Psalm 119:

- *I will delight in your statutes; I will not forget your word.* (verse 16)
- *Your testimonies are my delight; they are my counselors.* (verse 24)
- *Lead me in the path of your commandments, for I delight in it.* (verse 35)
- *for I find my delight in your commandments, which I love.* (verse 47)
- *I long for your salvation, O LORD, and your law is my delight.* (verse 174)

Psalm 119 uses the word "delight" 10 times in reference to God's Word. When you read the Bible with your children or students, will they sense in you a heartfelt delight? A holy reverence, mingled with sweet enjoyment? Think of how appealing it might be for them if they sensed in you an eager anticipation to open God's Word because you know there is life-giving treasure to be found!

> *The law of the LORD is perfect,*
> *reviving the soul;*
> *the testimony of the LORD is sure,*
> *making wise the simple;*
> *[8]the precepts of the LORD are right,*
> *rejoicing the heart;*
> *the commandment of the LORD is pure,*
> *enlightening the eyes;*

> [9]*the fear of the LORD is clean,*
> *enduring forever;*
> *the rules of the LORD are true,*
> *and righteous altogether.*
> [10]*More to be desired are they than gold,*
> *even much fine gold;*
> *sweeter also than honey*
> *and drippings of the honeycomb.*
> [11]*Moreover, by them is your servant warned;*
> *in keeping them there is great reward. (Psalm 19:7-11)*

This concept of delighting in God's Word really hit home one Sunday after I had taught a lesson. One of our pastors had been in the classroom that day. Afterward, he gently pulled me aside and commented, "You didn't seem to express joy in teaching God's Word today." His words and the conversation that followed led to a difficult but necessary *heart check*. I was teaching one thing to my students but conveying something very different through my demeanor.

> *Dry, unemotional, indifferent teaching about God—whether at home or at church—is a half-truth, at best. It says one thing about God and portrays another thing. It is inconsistent. It says that God is great, but teaches as if God is not great. Psalm 145:4 shows us another way: "One generation shall praise Your works to another." Let praises carry the truth to the next generation, because the aim of truth is praise.*[11]

3. Have a long-term strategy for acquainting children and youth with the entire Bible.

It wasn't until college that someone encouraged me to actually read through the entire Bible. Yes, I had grown up in the church, but I had never been exposed to vast portions of Scripture—especially the Old Testament, and the New Testament epistles. Hence, there were huge holes in my understanding of God, key people and events, what it means to live in newness of life, and the overall

---

11 John Piper. "One Generation Shall Praise Your Works to Another." March 19, 2000. desiringgod.org/messages/one-generation-shall-praise-your-works-to-another

unity of Scripture. The church, and especially the home, can work toward making sure that the next generation doesn't suffer this fate.

A simple way to get started is for parents to read the Bible[12] to their children, preferably on a daily basis. This doesn't need to be overly complicated or lengthy, especially with young children. When children are very young, start with a paragraph a day, or no more than a few minutes of reading. Gradually increase the duration as they get older. The goal is to begin to acquaint them with God's Word and slowly add more and more content over time.

Parents and other mentors, have you created an intentional, age-appropriate, long-term plan for doing this? Here are some suggestions:

- Choose a book of the Bible to read through. For younger children, consider beginning with one of the gospels. If necessary, leave out overly complex or confusing portions. Keep track of the portions you read. Upon completion of one book, start reading a new book of the Bible. Plot your progress from month to month and year to year.
- Use a Bible reading plan designed for children. For example, use *Exploring the Bible: A Bible Reading Plan for Kids* by David Murray, or see the Bible reading plan in *Meeting God in His Word: A Guide to Bible Reading and Prayer for Children* by Sally Michael (Truth78.org).
- Make use of time spent in the car with audio versions of the Bible. Children will pick up and remember more than you think.
- Modify a yearly reading plan developed for adults by choosing age-appropriate sections to read together. As children age and mature, add more and more portions of Scripture to read. Consider taking a one-year reading plan and doing it over the course of two years.

Whatever type of plan you use, remember to keep it short and simple for young children (5 to 10 minutes of reading) and choose a regular time and place that provides minimal distractions. Offer small incentives to keep children attentive.

---

12 While there is a good and helpful place for Bible story resources for children, I am referring to an actual Bible here and not a paraphrase version or storybook Bible.

Christian parents must prioritize the Bible above all other subjects. Yes, there are many subjects to teach our children, but teaching them to study the Bible is the most important by far. And communicating that priority to our children is the first and most essential step in that process. By our own example of personal Bible reading, by reading of the Bible together as a family, and by regular attendance at a Bible-focused church, we are sending a message that will make teaching them to study the Bible for themselves so much easier. If they see that we clearly view the Bible as the greatest book in the world, it's far more likely that they will want to read it for themselves.[13]

Whatever you do, make Bible reading a regular habit in your children's lives. Make it a high priority so that by the time your children, and all the children of your church, reach adulthood—they will have read the entire Bible.

4. Emphasize the whole counsel of God.

In the past few years, there has been a renewed focus on teaching children the entirety of Scripture from one main perspective, namely, teaching the redemptive storyline of the Bible from Genesis onward. Every text taught and every lesson presented tries to help children "see Jesus" and make a direct connection to His saving work on the cross. While there is much to commend and celebrate in this methodology, we must ask, is this the ONLY perspective of Bible reading and study our children and students need? Will it give them all the necessary categories for understanding the totality of what the Bible communicates?

It is essential that we give children all the necessary categories for understanding the sheer breadth and depth of Scripture, its historical context, the overarching redemptive narrative, and the essential doctrines of the Christian faith that must be adhered to and carefully guarded in each generation.

In Acts 20:27, Paul speaks about the importance of declaring the "whole counsel of God." What did he mean by this?

---
[13] David Murray. "How Can I Get My Kids to Read the Bible?" December 19, 2017. headhearthand.org/?s=how+can+I+get+my+kids+to+read+the+bible

> *What he must mean is that he taught the burden of the whole of God's revelation, the balance of things, leaving nothing out that was of primary importance, never ducking the hard bits, helping believers to grasp the whole counsel of God that they themselves would become better equipped to read their Bibles intelligently, comprehensively. It embraced*
> - *God's purposes in the history of redemption (truths to be believed and a God to be worshiped),*
> - *an unpacking of human origin, fall, redemption, and destiny (a worldview that shapes all human understanding and a Savior without whom there is no hope),*
> - *the conduct expected of God's people (commandments to be obeyed and wisdom to be pursued, both in our individual existence and in the community of the people of God), and*
> - *the pledges of transforming power both in this life and in the life to come (promises to be trusted and hope to be anticipated).*[14]

At Truth78, we have identified five theological perspectives or disciplines that help to highlight and communicate the whole counsel of God to children and youth. Here is a very brief overview:

1. Bible Survey and Book Studies

Introduces children to the key people, places, events, and themes of the Bible in chronological order so that they have a Bible foundation. As they grow in maturity, pursue more in-depth studies of individual books of the Bible.

2. Biblical Theology

Helps children to see and understand the overarching storyline of Scripture, whereby God progressively reveals His redemptive purposes, which come to their complete fulfillment in the person and work of Jesus Christ. By doing this, biblical theology emphasizes the unity of Scripture.

---

[14] D.A. Carson, contributing writer. *Preach the Word: Essays on Expository Preaching: In Honor of R. Kent Hughes.* Edited by Leland Ryken and Todd Wilson. (Wheaton, Ill.: Crossway Books, 2007), 177-178.

3. Systematic Theology

Children learn the Bible's teaching on the various essential doctrines of the Christian faith. Each doctrine is summarized based on the entirety of what Scripture teaches about it.

4. Gospel Proclamation

This provides children with an explicit and comprehensive presentation of the essential truths of the gospel, leading to a clear understanding of the person and work of Jesus Christ and what it means to respond in true repentance and faith.

5. Moral and Ethical Instruction

Gives children a proper understanding of the nature, role, and importance of God's laws and commands, the wisdom literature, and the moral and ethical teachings of Jesus and the apostles. This understanding is important for seeing God's righteousness and our desperate need for Christ, and for walking in newness of life.

During the scope of our children's biblical education, these should be presented and interwoven in a way that gives a proper balance. For example, our children will be not well served if they are repeatedly taught from a biblical theology perspective but do not have a good grasp of systematic theology and the doctrines that define the Christian life.

Teaching the whole counsel of God is a huge endeavor and is best accomplished when both the church and home partner together. The church must carefully look at its curricula's scope and sequence[15] and other teaching resources and ask: Over the course of our students' time in our classrooms, will they be taught the whole counsel of God? Are we equipping parents with the resources and encouragement they need to do this? One resource I highly recommend that will serve both church and home in this regard is Sally Michael's *More Than a Story* (Old and New Testament volumes). It uniquely incorporates all of these theological perspectives in an engaging, child-friendly manner.

---

15 Go to Truth78.org/scope-sequence-explanation to read about how our curricula have been developed to teach the whole counsel of God.

5. Teach children to rightly read and interpret Scripture by equipping them with age-appropriate Bible study skills.

Most people are familiar with the old proverb: If you give a man a fish, you feed him for a day; if you teach a man to fish, you feed him for a lifetime. This proverb can serve as a reminder about how important it is to teach our children how to "fish," as it were, in regard to God's Word. Too often we give children "fish." We serve up the Bible lesson, telling them what to think, while neglecting to teach them the necessary tools and training to rightly read and study the Bible for *themselves*.

In his article, "How to Teach Your Kids to Study the Bible," Joe Carter gives this very short but helpful summary of what is involved.

> *...while encouraging our children to read the Bible and teaching them how to do it well are necessary tasks, they are not sufficient for spiritual development. We also need to teach them how to study Scripture so that they "may be thoroughly equipped for every good work" (2 Tim. 3:17).*
>
> *When we study the Bible, though, we slow down to focus on the meaning of the text. We read and reread shorter units of text and spend more time focusing on specific words, clauses, verses, and paragraphs...*
>
> *The essence of Bible study is asking questions of the text to discover the meaning God intended. Of the many profitable ways to study the Bible, one that many from preteens to Old Testament scholars have found to be particularly helpful is the inductive Bible study method. The inductive study method is an investigative approach to the Bible using three basic components:*
>
> - *Observation: What does the text say?*
> - *Interpretation: What does the text mean?*
> - *Application: How does the meaning of the text apply to life?*[16]

---

16 Joe Carter. "How to Teach Your Kids to Study the Bible." July 13, 2019. thegospelcoalition.org/article/teach-kids-study-bible/

Our children and students need to know how to rightly read *and* study the Bible.¹⁷ Unfortunately, there has been a growing tendency for Sunday school classrooms to focus more on hands-on-learning (engaging and fun activities designed to create a physically active environment) rather than on active minds. What is meant by *active minds*? Here is a brief description by Sally Michael:

> *Active learning involves children's minds interacting with the subject matter; they are thinking—discovering, imagining, questioning, organizing, analyzing, evaluating, drawing conclusions—and applying the material.*

Our Sunday school rooms and homes need to prioritize this kind of learning, the "subject matter" being the Bible itself. Part 2 of this booklet, "Equipping and Training Children to Read and Study the Bible" will provide guidance on how to go about doing this for specific age categories.

That being said, this is no easy task. After all, it's much easier to simply give children information and have them regurgitate answers back to us. It is much more difficult—but ultimately much more fruitful—to teach them how to actively engage with God's Word for themselves. It is also absolutely necessary for the Christian life.

> *Christian faithfulness requires the development of the believer's intellectual capacities in order that we may understand the Christian faith, develop habits of Christian thought, form intuitions that are based upon biblical truth, and live in faithfulness to all that Christ teaches. This is no easy task, to be sure. Just as Christian discipleship requires growth and development, intellectual faithfulness requires a lifetime of devoted study, consecrated thinking, and analytical reflection.*¹⁸

---

17 Here are two articles that state the importance of preparing the next generation for serious study of the Bible: "A Compelling Reason for Rigorous Training of the Mind" by John Piper (desiringgod.org/articles/a-compelling-reason-for-rigorous-training-of-the-mind), and "The Glory of God and the Life of the Mind" by Albert Mohler (albertmohler.com/2010/11/12/the-glory-of-god-and-the-life-of-the-mind)
18 R. Albert Mohler, Jr. "The Glory of God in the Life of the Mind." November 12, 2010, albertmohler.com/2010/11/12/the-glory-of-god-and-the-life-of-the-mind

6. Guide and implore children to rightly respond to and apply God's Word.

Here are some sobering words from Jesus,

> "This people honors me with their lips, but their heart is far from me;" (Matthew 15:8)

Jesus spoke these words to the highly religious people of His day, men who had vast amounts of Scripture memorized, men who were the church leaders of their day. But their hearts were ice cold and hard as stone. We should be mindful of these words every time we lead a devotion or teach a Bible lesson to our children and students. If we merely seek to instill more and more Bible knowledge into the mind, without regard to the heart and will, we may inadvertently encourage them to become little *Pharisees*.

Let's look again at the definition of biblical literacy that was offered earlier:

> *Biblical literacy is acquainting our children with the breadth, depth, and authority of Scripture so that they would come to know, honor, and treasure the God of the Bible, setting their hope in Christ alone, and be trained and equipped to live as His faithful disciples for the glory of God.*

This definition makes clear that biblical literacy aims at...

> Instructing the mind → engaging the heart → and influencing the will

Knowledge of the Bible has as its goal, *spiritual transformation.* Therefore, we should never leave the heart and will untouched when reading and studying the Bible. What does this involve in practical terms? It will involve things such as:

- Asking questions about the text that guide and encourage children to ponder a sincere and genuine response that is pleasing to God. What is God commanding them to personally feel, desire, trust, treasure, be, say, or do?
- Helping children discern, recognize, and understand the problem of their sin before a holy God and their utter help-

lessness to save themselves: *What did this Bible story show about the Israelites' hearts? Why were they grumbling against God? Do you ever grumble? What does this show you about your own heart? Can you fix your own heart? Why not? Can God? How has He provided the perfect solution for your sin problem? What does God's Word say you must do?*

- Emphasizing that believing in God's Word, depending upon it, and obeying it are necessary for lasting joy. *This is what God's Word says will bring you the most happiness. Do you trust what God says? Why would obeying God in this situation bring you more joy?*
- Pointing over and over again to the surpassing greatness and worth of Jesus. Jesus is our only hope! *Do you truly love and trust Jesus as your Savior? How is this shown in your life? How are you growing to become more and more like Him?*
- Suggesting further steps to help them act upon a specific passage. *This verse tells us to be kind, tenderhearted, and forgiving because of the great kindness, love, and forgiveness God has shown to us through Jesus. Is there someone you have a hard time being kind to? Is there someone you need to forgive? How could you act on this?*

Here is a final but important point to keep in mind because it is not simply about imploring our children and students to rightly respond with their hearts and wills. Teachers and parents need to be living examples of how trusting in Christ and loving Him as your greatest treasure changes everything.

I have to admit that, especially when my children were young, I often taught the Bible to them with the mindset, "*They* need to hear this and be changed by it. How can I use this passage to challenge, rebuke, and correct *them*?"...always with *them* in mind. But what did they observe about the amount of time mom spent in the Word herself? What did they see and hear from me when the day didn't go as planned, sickness came, the car broke down, or I had conflict with my husband? Did my words and actions demonstrate a love for Christ and humble submission to His Word? Did I demonstrate unshakable confidence in His promises?

Our homes [and classrooms] *are the laboratory of life for our children. They will believe that Christian faith is the genuine article if we know God—not just know about God. As children grow to young adulthood in our churches, they are searching desperately for a faith that has the warmth and vitality of close relationship with the living God, and the sure footing of sound doctrine that will stand the storms of life. Relationship with God is the passionate assurance that the Sovereign God of the Bible can be known by his people in all the experiences of life. Our relationship with God will beckon our children to draw near to him as their source of comfort and rest.*[19]

7. Instill in children the need for humble dependence on the Holy Spirit as they read and study the Bible.

Of all the changes I have experienced in the classroom in the past 30 years, one of the most significant was our pastor, David Michael, encouraging each and every Sunday school team to pray together every week before the children arrived. Those 5 to 10 minutes spent in earnest prayer had a profound effect on our teaching, the atmosphere of the class time, and the demeanor of the children as we studied the Scriptures together. As a teacher it gave me humble confidence in what God might be pleased to sovereignly do in the lives of my students—in spite of my imperfect teaching.

> *"But the Helper, the Holy Spirit, whom the Father will send in my name, he will teach you all things and bring to your remembrance all that I have said to you." (John 14:26)*

In order to truly understand, embrace, and apply God's Word, we and our children need the Holy Spirit. The Spirit is necessary to awaken sinners to Christ, reveal and illuminate the truth, and empower us to love, trust, and obey Him. We are utterly dependent on the Spirit's help in all these ways.

Therefore, as we open the Scriptures with our children and students, we should make clear this dependency. We shouldn't simply treat

---

[19] Tedd and Margy Tripp. *Instructing a Child's Heart*. (Wapwallopen, Penn.: Shepherd Press, 2008), 29.

time in the Bible as if it is one more academic pursuit amongst others. One easy way to do this is pray before and after reading Scripture. For young children, it can be a simple prayer, echoing the psalmist, *"Dear heavenly Father, open our eyes that we might see wondrous things from Your law"* (Psalm 119:18). For older children, you could even consider singing a simple song before reading and studying the Word. "Speak, O Lord" (by Keith Getty and Stuart Townend) reflects a humble plea for God's help, as seen in this verse, for example:

> *Speak, O Lord, as we come to You*
> *To receive the food of Your Holy Word*
> *Take Your truth, plant it deep in us*
> *Shape and fashion us in Your likeness...*[20]

8. Integrate and connect biblical truth to all of life.

In college, I painfully trudged through a required year of calculus. Now, more than 40 years later, I still don't understand why I needed to learn calculus. It seemed to have no direct, personal application to my life. And when you can't see the importance of studying something, you are less likely to pursue it with any interest or gusto.

But what's so amazing about the Bible is how it applies to EVERYTHING in life—schoolwork, sports, friendships, possessions, movies, the environment, sickness, bullies, evil, war, politics...and on and on. We must show our children and students how biblical truth is like a lens for seeing and interpreting *all of life*. No subject is outside its authoritative domain.

> *God is not just the Savior of souls, He is also the Lord of creation. One way we acknowledge His Lordship is by interpreting every aspect of creation in light of His truth. God's Word becomes a set of glasses offering a new perspective on all our thoughts and actions.*[21]

---

20 Keith Getty and Stuart Townend. "Speak, O Lord." (ThankYou Music, administered by worshiptogether.com songs, 2005).
21 Nancy R. Pearcey. *Total Truth: Liberating Christianity from Its Cultural Captivity*. (Wheaton, Ill.: Crossway Books, 2005), 24.

Look for opportunities to do this in the daily rhythm of life. When reading Scripture, guide children in discovering these connections. For example, after reading a passage together, relate it to something your child has experienced:

> *The heavens declare the glory of God, and the sky above proclaims his handiwork. [2]Day to day pours out speech, and night to night reveals knowledge. (Psalm 19:1-2)*

> *Remember what we saw in the sky yesterday after the rainstorm? Who made that rainbow? What does God want you to see in the beauty of that rainbow? How does a rainbow "speak" about God's greatness?*

> *What kind of things did we see in the night sky last night? How do the moon, stars, and planets help us know something about God?*

Also, help your children and students see how timely and relevant Scripture is in relating to their ordinary, everyday interactions with others. For example:

> *Let no corrupting talk come out of your mouths, but only such as is good for building up, as fits the occasion, that it may give grace to those who hear. (Ephesians 4:29)*

Ask your children and students to ponder how this verse should guide their words toward siblings and friends, and their interactions on social media. What would submission to God's truth look like? What does this verse tell us to do? What is the good and right way to talk? How shouldn't we talk to others?

In other words, when questions and situations arise ask, "What does the Bible have to say about this?" The more we help children do this, the more they will see the amazing sufficiency of the Bible. This application of God's truth to ALL of life becomes especially pertinent as they grow older and encounter the world's aggressive and radically unbiblical views.

> *What does God's Word say about how the world came into existence? Why is the world's explanation foolish and wrong?*

> *Can a boy become a girl? Can a girl become a boy? What does the Bible say about this? What evidence has God given us to show that His Word is true regarding this?*

Our children and youth need answers to the hard questions (Colossians 2:8; 2 Corinthians 10:5). We need to be ready to demonstrate to them that the Bible is sufficient and trustworthy. It provides a sure, unshakable foundation on which to stand firm with joyful confidence.

9. Foster a partnership that promotes biblical literacy in both home and church.

Have you ever tried to look through only one eyepiece in a set of binoculars? You will get a clear image, but the image will be very limited in its scope, greatly reducing the usefulness of the binoculars. The two eyepieces have been carefully designed to work in sync so that we can see a clear image that is broader in scope. In a similar way, God designed the church and home to be like the two eyepieces that are meant to work *in sync*—in partnership—with one another in order to offer a more expansive instruction in the holy Word of God.

At Truth78, we describe this vital partnership as follows:

> We believe that God has called both the church and home to raise up the next generations to know, honor, and treasure God through Jesus Christ. We believe this is best accomplished through a strategic, loving partnership between the church and home. This partnership affirms the role and responsibility of church leadership to provide encouragement and training for parents, and also to provide formal instruction for children and youth. This partnership affirms that parents, by proximity, opportunity, and God's design, bear a unique responsibility for nurturing their children's faith (Deuteronomy 6:4-7; Psalm 78:1-8; Matthew 28:18-20; Ephesians 4:11-13).[22]

Individually, church and home each have an important role in guiding children to know, trust, and treasure God's Word. But the scope and impact will be far greater when church and home are intentionally working together. So here are some basic questions to ask:

---

22 For more information, see: Truth78.org/partnering-with-parents

- What formal biblical instruction is the church providing for children and youth? Is there a well-thought-out scope and sequence designed to declare the whole counsel of God? Are teachers and volunteers being equipped and trained to work toward that goal?
- What are parents doing in the home to instruct children from the Scriptures and nurture their faith? What resources are being recommended and used for this purpose? How is the church inspiring, encouraging, resourcing, and training parents for this role?
- Are the church and home in sync regarding the vision, mission, and goal? Do the resources used and the philosophy of instruction in both the church and home complement and reinforce one another?

10. Devote and prioritize the necessary time required to do points 1-9.

As life gets busier and busier, the time devoted to reading and studying the Bible can easily become crowded out, especially in the home. Even good and necessary educational pursuits—math, history, science, language arts—can serve to diminish time given to instructing our children in the Scriptures. Parents, carefully consider these questions posed by Chap Bettis:

> *The apostle John expressed his heart for his spiritual children when he wrote, "I have no greater joy than to hear that my children are walking in the truth" (3 John 4). Here lies the crux of the matter: The first battleground of family discipleship is not my child's heart—it is my heart. Each parent must decide whether he is more concerned that his child be accepted into Heaven, or "Harvard." We all have "Harvards"—those worldly successes we desire for our children, but the question remains, "Which is most important to me?" Each parent must finish the sentence "I have no greater joy than…" I would emphasize here that the challenge of priorities is often not the good versus the bad, rather, the good versus the better. Given a finite amount of time, energy, and money, what will you choose?*[23]

---

23 Chap Bettis. *The Disciple-Making Parent: A Comprehensive Guidebook for Raising Your Children to Love and Follow Jesus Christ.* (Providence County, R.I.: Diamond Hill Publishing, 2016), 17.

The same type of questions must be asked of the church. In the past several decades, I have witnessed a dramatic *decrease* in the amount of time and attention given to formal Bible instruction for children and youth. Just one generation ago, many churches offered formal teaching for children on Sunday mornings and evenings, plus a mid-week class. That being said, my children benefited from about 150 hours of instruction every year. However, today, not only are many Sunday school classes meeting for fewer and fewer weeks during the year, but many are also meeting for a shorter duration of time. Furthermore, within that shortened time frame, other activities are crowding out time spent in the Scriptures. Suffice it to say, some churches are offering children only about 50 hours of biblical instruction per year—one third the time my own children received![24]

Do we need to readjust our priorities and give more time to what is most important? Both the home and the church must prayerfully consider both the *quantity* and *quality* of our children's biblical instruction. Without adequate quantity (time), we will be hard-pressed to offer the kind of quality needed to teach the next generations the most important truths in the universe.

Final Thoughts

One Sunday morning after teaching the Bible lesson, I was approached by a seven-year-old girl who had a simple but surprisingly profound question for me: "Mrs. Nelson, is it possible for the Bible to become an idol?" Unbeknownst to her, that question reflects a wider criticism aimed at many conservative, reformed churches and Christians who are accused of being so absorbed in what's in the Bible—its content, doctrines, etc.—that a genuine and vibrant relationship with Christ is minimized. They claim that the Bible becomes the object of worship instead of God Himself. But this kind of criticism fails to fully embrace the totality of what the Bible is. So, how did I respond to that inquisitive seven-year-old? I asked questions such as, "Who is speaking to us in the Bible? Who do we

---

24 See: "A Plea to Pastors for More Sunday School" November 4, 2021, Truth78.org/blog/post/a-plea-to-pastors-for-more-sunday-school

come to know through the Bible?..." John Frame gives a wonderful summation regarding the *relational* quality of the Bible:

> ...*the personal presence of God always accompanies the Word, speaking the Word to our hearts. Where the Word is, God is, and where God is, the Word is. We should never try to seek fellowship with God apart from the Word. And when we do hear or read the Word, we should understand that we are entering the temple of God himself.*[25]

In other words, the Bible gives us the very means of knowing and communing with the one true God. The Bible enables, informs, and nurtures our relationship with the triune God. To minimize the reading, study of, and meditation on the Bible, is to minimize the power of God's presence in our lives. Over the years, this has been proven true in my own life. When I have neglected time in the Word, I feel more distant from the presence of Christ. But time in the Word brings about a renewed closeness and comfort as I hear His voice speaking to me through His Word. Therefore, as we teach the Bible to children, it's essential that we guide them in both the doctrinal and relational aspects of Scripture. We must teach the Bible in such a way as to implore them to, and pray that they, above all, would come to know, trust, treasure, and follow Jesus all the days of their lives!

> *Every family* [and church] *should have some intentional and structured times in which the children are taught about what the Scriptures contain. We must faithfully urge them to believe the things we have taught... None of this will be enough unless they entrust themselves to Jesus Christ. If they are to be partakers of eternal life, they must trust in this Jesus Christ who saves. Our children must receive Him, turn to Him, hold fast to Him, and rest in Him alone for salvation. Ultimately, the work of the Holy Spirit must transform our children into people who rest in Christ alone for salvation. Our role is to bring them the gospel and urge them to embrace Christ the Savior.*[26]

---

[25] John M. Frame. *Systematic Theology: An Introduction to Christian Belief*. (Phillipsburg, NJ: P&R Publishing, 2013), 531.
[26] Tedd Tripp. "A Child's Call to Conversion: Faith as a Christian Mark." October 1, 2010. ligonier.org/learn/articles/childs-call-conversion-faith-christian-mark

Part 2
Equipping and Training Children to Read and Study the Bible

It began as an experiment and a challenge. Could we encourage and guide a classroom of 30 first-grade children—many of whom could not even read yet—to readily and eagerly look up a passage of Scripture during our Sunday school lesson? Furthermore, could we actually teach them how to carefully study the passage in order to discover its meaning? Some teachers and parents thought this wasn't doable. But then, weeks later, the day came. I wrote a Bible reference on the whiteboard. Next, there were 30 heads intently bent over their Bibles, fingers quickly ruffling through the pages. One by one, children excitedly jumped up from their seats with huge smiles on their faces. They found it!

Even 20-some years later, I can still recall that day vividly in my mind. It brought tears to my eyes then, and it still does now. Yes, it may seem like a very small accomplishment, but it was a very important one that was merely the beginning, Lord willing, in a lifelong pursuit of becoming fully acquainted with God's Word. But it didn't happen by accident. It was accomplished by setting specific goals, and guiding and helping children to reach those goals.

Using this Section

This section is designed to introduce some age-appropriate goals for reading and studying Scripture, practical tools for helping children reach those goals, and specific examples of doing so. You will also notice that each new category builds upon the previous one. So if, for example, you are teaching eight-year-olds, you should read what skills were ideally introduced for the younger ages. If your eight-year-olds were not taught those foundational skills, you may need to adjust your expectations accordingly. While acknowledging that there are some children who may face unique obstacles and need extra help and time, most children, when properly guided and encouraged, will be able to achieve these goals within the noted age categories.

It is also important to note that some study tools and examples are presented within the context of a classroom setting. This tends to be a more challenging environment in which to pursue biblical literacy and one in which genuine Bible study is often minimized. That said, the tools and examples given are readily applicable to the home.

Additional Tips for Helping Children and Students Read and Study the Bible

- As much as possible, provide an environment free of unnecessary distractions. Some children are especially hindered by unrelated visual and audible distractions.
- Clearly communicate expectations regarding the duration of the session, general attentiveness, responding to and asking questions, etc.
- Before and after reading and studying the Scriptures, pray, emphasizing the need for the Spirit's help in rightly understanding and responding to God's Word.
- Make sure that you are all using the same translation of the Bible. This is extremely important especially for younger children. Choose a good translation that will take them into adulthood (e.g., English Standard Version). Have extra copies of the Bible available for children who don't have one.
- Set realistic expectations for each child—children of the same age can vary widely in their reading and cognitive abilities.
- Offer incentives and rewards for reaching certain milestones.
- Always encourage children toward new goals.

- Repeatedly emphasize that biblical literacy is not simply *knowing* the Bible. The goal is to know, trust, treasure, and follow Jesus. The ability to quickly look up verses and read and answer questions proficiently doesn't mean a child is more spiritually mature than a child who struggles with these skills. In fact, the opposite may be true. In other words, strive to inspire *spiritual* transformation.

One last note: Over the course of their biblical instruction, children should be introduced to and repeatedly reminded of verses that describe the Bible itself, its innate qualities. A list of some suggested verses can be found in the appendix.

Reading and Studying the Bible:
Preschool (Ages 3-4)

These years are too often overlooked in terms of biblical literacy. However, they provide a prime opportunity to introduce children to an audible form of biblical literacy, one that will serve to give them a head start before they begin to read and study the Bible.

Main Goals
- Introduce children to the main people and events of the Bible in a chronological manner (Bible survey).
- Highlight the main foundational theological truths presented in Scripture.
- Slowly acquaint children with the actual language of Scripture.
- Begin simple Bible memory.

Content to Emphasize and Methods to Employ[27]
- **Teach chronologically through the Old and New Testaments through telling simple Bible stories that highlight the key narratives of Scripture.** Make sure to include a wide array of stories, even some of the more difficult ones.
- **Tell Bible stories in a manner that is age-appropriate and yet carefully and accurately conveys the true meaning of the text.** At this age, focus on communicating one or two main ideas presented in the text using simple language. Your demeanor and tone should reflect that of the text (e.g., joyful, sad, surprising, fearful, confident, etc.).
- **Use an open Bible as you teach and emphasize that the story you are sharing comes from God's Word.** Before

---
[27] I strongly recommend using the Truth78 preschool curricula *He Established a Testimony* (stories from the Old Testament) and *He Has Spoken By His Son* (stories from the New Testament). The accompanying workbooks for each curriculum are ideal for use in the home (Truth78.org).

summarizing the story in your own words, point to where the story is found in the Bible.
- **Look for opportunities to read directly from the text, even if it is only one or two verses.** When you do this, preface it by saying something like, "This is what the Bible says. Listen very carefully to what God says!"
- **State, repeat, and review common key theological truths that are revealed in the stories** (e.g., God loves His people, God is strong, God is King over everyone, God knows everything, we must love God most, people are sinful and disobey God, God saves His people, etc.).
- **Use visual aids to help children understand the historical nature of people and events, as well as the order of each** (e.g., a picture timeline).
- **Give concrete, everyday examples to help them grasp more abstract concepts** (e.g., When daddy and mommy tell you to not touch a hot stove, is that a good rule? Does it show that they love you and want to protect you from getting hurt? God has rules, too. He gives us rules because He loves us.)
- **Make simple connections and point out progression in the individual stories as well as the Bible as a whole.** For example, after telling children the story of Adam and Eve's sin from Genesis 3, you could state the following progression:

God created Adam and Eve, and God put them in the garden to live. God gave them a special rule about one tree in the garden: "Don't eat from this tree or you will die." God's rules are always good. Adam and Eve must obey God's rules. Did they obey God? No. Adam and Eve did not obey God. They ate from that one tree.

Questions to Ask:

Would God be happy with Adam and Eve? No. Why not? Because they disobeyed His rule. That was wrong. What would happen to Adam and Eve? Yes, they would die.

- **Use the foundational theological themes highlighted throughout the Bible stories to present a simple and consistent gospel message.** It is not necessary that the children fully comprehend every concept at this age, but they are hearing the essential truths of the gospel. For example:
  - *God is holy; He never sins. He created us to love and obey Him always. But people disobey God—we are sinners. God is right to punish sin.*
  - *God loves us and is patient and kind. God made a way to save sinners.*
  - *God sent Jesus to us. Jesus is God's Son. He never sinned. He always obeyed God.*
  - *Jesus died to take our punishment. He died to save us. After He died, Jesus came alive again! Believe in Jesus and you will be saved!*
- **Encourage Bible memory in the class and at home.**[28] Preschoolers have an amazing capacity to memorize. Not only does Bible memory acquaint children with more Scripture—it also highlights the fact that God's Word is so important it is worth remembering. God's Word is a powerful weapon for fighting sin. It gives us hope and joy. Simple verses that are also applicable to their daily lives are especially beneficial. For example:
  - *When I am afraid, I put my trust in you. (Psalm 56:3)*
  - *Children, obey your parents in the Lord, for this is right. (Ephesians 6:1)*
  - *For the wages of sin is death, but the free gift of God is eternal life in Christ Jesus our Lord. (Romans 6:23)*

---

28 For preschool Bible memory resources see *Foundation Verses* at Truth78.org.

Reading and Studying the Bible:
Kindergarten (Ages 5-6)

Kindergarten is a transitional time for children. Some are already beginning to read, while many others are still exclusively visual and auditory learners. If you are teaching in a classroom setting, be sensitive to and address both groups.

Main Goals
- Learn and memorize the books of the Bible in proper order.
- Emphasize the truthfulness, authority, and necessity of Scripture. Explore the redemptive storyline of Scripture.
- Begin to examine simple verses for context and meaning.

Content to Emphasize and Methods to Employ
- **Choose a song or game to help children learn the books of the Bible.** Many ideas are available online. Choose one that is easy to sing or play, and repeat it often.
- **Regularly remind children that the Bible is given to us by God Himself and is always true, right, and for our good.** Emphasize that, as much as we need food and water, we need God's Word even more! Only the Bible can give us what is most important to be happy.
- **Increasingly, read more directly from the Bible.** For example, read an entire paragraph/short narrative so they start to recognize the *language* of the Bible—letting the Bible speak for itself. Then go back and explain it using appropriate visual aids if possible.
- **Write out key Bible terms and give simple and accurate definitions.** Doing this will help expand the children's comprehension of Bible terminology. For example:
    - Almighty → *God is all-powerful.*
    - Faithful → *God keeps His promises.*

- Eternal life → *living forever in heaven with God*

  Be careful to define Bible terms simply but accurately. For example, it would be inaccurate to define "sin" as "mistakes." The essence of sin is not unintentional acts or thoughtless carelessness. Defining sin as "disobeying God," while not expansive in meaning, rightly defines the moral essence of sin.

- **Write out key verses and ask related questions.** All children, especially visually oriented learners, will be more motivated to become further engaged with the text when you actually point to Bible words and explain their meaning. For example:

  "For the Son of Man came to seek and to save the lost." (Luke 19:10)

  "Son of Man" is another name for Jesus. "Seek" means to look for something. In this verse, "the lost" are people who are sinners. So this verse is saying that Jesus came to look for sinners and save them.

- **Personalize the Bible so that children understand the message is for them.** Because the goal of biblical literacy is spiritual transformation, we must guide and encourage children to see that the text applies to them personally. Using Luke 19:10 again, state "These words of Jesus are for you and me also. You and I are sinners. We need Jesus to seek after us and save us."

- **Emphasize the authority of the Bible as you teach—the Bible is to be believed and obeyed.** Here is a very familiar verse:

  Children, obey your parents in the Lord, for this is right. (Ephesians 6:1)

  Questions to Ask:

  Is God asking if you would like to obey your parents? No. God is not asking you if you feel like obeying your parents. This is a command, and God wants you to obey this command. It is for your good.

Reading Scripture with this mindset is crucial. Scripture should be read asking two basic questions: *What does this text mean?* And *how does God call on me to respond?*

- **Emphasize the redemptive storyline of the Bible.** If the preschool years have introduced children to a wide array of key chronological Bible stories, we can now focus on selected stories and Scriptures to help children grasp how the Bible's narrative has a progressive redemptive theme that finds its fulfillment in Jesus.[29]
- **Continue to encourage Bible memory.**

---

[29] See *God's Gospel* (Truth78.org/gods-gospel).

Reading and Studying the Bible:
1st-2nd Grade (Ages 7-8)

By the time most children reach this age group, they are becoming increasingly proficient in their reading skills. This is an ideal time to stress more hands-on, interactive Bible skills. So a priority should be that each child have his own Bible. In the classroom, make sure to communicate this priority to parents and offer assistance if necessary. Consider the following when choosing a Bible for children:

- Make sure it's a *real* Bible, with the full text of both Old and New Testaments.
- Find a Bible with a font and format that is easy to read and with an overall structure that is easy to use. Small font size is difficult for children.
- Look for a minimal number of cross references, footnotes, and commentary.
- Simple realistic illustrations, maps, and other charts and graphs may be helpful.

Main Goals

- Learn how to find things in the Bible.
- Equip them with basic Bible study tools for examining a simple passage of Scripture.
- Expand their knowledge of God's character (His attributes) and how we are to respond to Him.
- Introduce a short, comprehensive overview of the gospel.

Content to Emphasize and Methods to Employ

- **Introduce games and hands-on activities to help children visibly recognize/read the titles of the books of the Bible.** As mentioned previously, books of the Bible songs are a great way to initially teach children the names and order. But now they can be taught to recognize/read the titles of

books of the Bible as they appear in their Bibles. (See the appendix for some specific games and activities.)
- **Give explicit instructions for finding a specific passage in the Bible.** Begin by writing the Bible reference for an easy-to-read/easy-to-find passage on a whiteboard or large piece of paper. Example: Exodus 2:10. Explain that this is a kind of *address*, telling us where to find the verse/s in the Bible. Highlight which is the book name, chapter, and verse. Then, have them find the book of Exodus in their Bibles. Next, help them to find the correct chapter and verse. Over time, practice using a variety of passages from throughout the Bible. Additionally, show them how to use their Bible's table of contents.
- **Guide children in looking up one or more simple passages during the lesson time.** While this can be time consuming, especially for beginning readers, it's an invaluable tool for leading children to interact with the Scriptures being taught. Here are some ideas for doing this in a timely manner:
    - Assign the book and chapter before the students gather for the lesson (e.g., in their small groups, when they first arrive in class). Give them a slip of paper to use as a bookmark. During the lesson, have them open to the passage and give the verse/s number/s.
    - Have adults sit with children, especially those who will need more help.
    - Sword Drills can be a fun activity to encourage students to quickly look up a passage. Be sure to encourage children regardless of their reading ability. (See the appendix for instructions.)
- **Demonstrate how to examine a simple passage of Scripture in order to understand its meaning and make personal application.** Even if you have had the students look up the passage in their Bibles, it is helpful to write out a short passage and guide them by asking specific questions that will help them to understand the meaning. Here are two examples:

- *Isaiah 44:24b—..."'I am the LORD, who made all things, who alone stretched out the heavens, who spread out the earth by myself,"*

  Who is speaking in this verse? (Point to "the LORD.")

  Did God make just SOME things? What word does God use to show that He didn't make just SOME things? (Point to "all.")

  Did God have help making all things? What words does God use to show that He didn't need any help? ("by myself")

- *Psalm 103:13-14—As a father shows compassion to his children, so the LORD shows compassion to those who fear him. ¹⁴For he knows our frame; he remembers that we are dust.*

  What do fathers show to their children? [compassion] *What is compassion?* [loving care]

  Who does God show compassion to? [to those who fear Him] *That means everyone who is trusting in Jesus. Look at the last part of the verse. What does it mean that God knows our "frame" and remembers that we are "dust"? Is dust strong or weak?*

  Why is it a good thing that God keeps in mind that we are weak?

  As these questions demonstrate, you are helping children to discover the basic elements of the passage. By directing your questions toward certain words and comparisons, you are zooming in on key truths that help to simplify and summarize the verse. (Note about pronouns: Make sure children understand who the "he," "his," etc. are referring to in a passage.)

- **Expand the children's scope of biblical texts by including passages throughout the Bible.** We want our children to become acquainted with the whole Bible. When possible, and in keeping with your overall study, include texts from a

variety of books. At home, this is best done by using a Bible reading plan or even by creating your own.
- **Use a variety of texts to demonstrate the greatness of God's character and how we are to respond to Him.** At this age, it is especially important to show how the Bible answers three basic questions: *Who is God? What is God like? And how should we respond to God?* For example, have the children look at these three verses and ask them if they see a common word/s used to describe something about what God is like:
  - *1 Chronicles 29:11a—Yours, O LORD, is the greatness and the power and the glory and the victory and the majesty,*
  - *Job 37:23a—The Almighty—we cannot find him; he is great in power;*
  - *Jeremiah 32:17—"Ah, Lord GOD! It is you who have made the heavens and the earth by your great power and by your outstretched arm! Nothing is too hard for you."*

  These verses all state a key attribute of God: He is great in power. He is almighty. By using a variety of texts, the children can see how this important truth is displayed throughout Scripture. Additionally, as you read Scripture, have children note passages that call for specific responses. For example, after reading these verses, examine verses that demonstrate how we should respond.
  - *1 Peter 5:6a—Humble yourselves, therefore, under the mighty hand of God...*
  - *Psalm 150:2—Praise him for his mighty deeds; praise him according to his excellent greatness!*
  - *Isaiah 41:10—fear not, for I am with you; be not dismayed, for I am your God; I will strengthen you, I will help you, I will uphold you with my righteous right hand.*
- **Introduce a short, comprehensive overview of the gospel.** By this time, children should have been introduced to key attributes of God, foundational Bible doctrines, and the redemptive storyline of the Bible. These can be succinctly summarized to provide children with a more comprehen-

sive understanding of the gospel. Truth78 has developed various simple resources to highlight 10 essential gospel truths.[30] (See the appendix for a list of 10 essential truths of the gospel.)

- **Incorporate a Bible reading plan at home.** This can be done as part of family devotions or by giving a child a specific plan to read on his own or with the help of a parent or older sibling.[31]
- **Begin a more rigorous Bible memory program.** This would ideally include the entire family and church. For example, you could use the Fighter Verses™ program from Truth78 (Truth78.org).

---

30 For simple resources to highlight essential gospel truths, see: Truth78.org/gospel-resources
31 For example: David Murray's *Exploring the Bible: A Bible Reading Plan for Kids* or Sally Michael's *Meeting God in His Word: A Guide to Bible Reading and Prayer for Children* (Truth78.org)

Reading and Studying the Bible:
3rd-5th Grade (Ages 9-11)

Most children are ready for more serious Bible study at this age. They can begin to absorb and comprehend more Scripture, and they have enough emotional maturity to be able to ponder spiritual concepts and the implications for their lives.

Main Goals
- Introduce more substantial texts to read and study (e.g., an entire narrative/story).
- Demonstrate how to use basic inductive Bible study skills.
- Explain how the Bible is organized.
- Acquaint them with helps often found in Bibles (e.g., introductory notes, glossary/dictionary, commentary, cross references, etc.)
- Point out the unity of Scripture from Old Testament to New Testament.
- Guide and implore children to respond in faith and Spirit-empowered obedience.

Content to Emphasize and Methods to Employ
- **Substantially increase the amount of text children interact with in a given lesson.** Children should be encouraged and expected to interact with more and more text, including reading passages aloud. Their Bibles should be open more often than not.
- **In the classroom, carefully choose who will be reading the text/s—the teacher or the students.** Be strategic about which passages and how many passages you assign the students to read aloud. Time does not usually permit every student to look up every passage in the lesson. If you have several different texts in a lesson, consider assigning texts to

students right before the lesson, giving each student time to look up the text. Then, call on them to read their text during the lesson. Note: Not all children feel comfortable reading aloud in a classroom setting. Do not force it.

- **Use guided questions and explanations to help the children properly interpret the text.**
- **Have them make specific observations—noting key words, phrases, patterns, and contexts.** Again, this skill was introduced in a very basic way in first and second grade, but it can now be expanded upon. Here is an example:

Have them turn to the parable of the unforgiving servant from Matthew 18:23-35.

Matthew 18:23-35—"Therefore the kingdom of heaven may be compared to a king who wished to settle accounts with his servants. ^{24}When he began to settle, one was brought to him who owed him ten thousand talents. ^{25}And since he could not pay, his master ordered him to be sold, with his wife and children and all that he had, and payment to be made. ^{26}So the servant fell on his knees, imploring him, 'Have patience with me, and I will pay you everything.' ^{27}And out of pity for him, the master of that servant released him and forgave him the debt. ^{28}But when that same servant went out, he found one of his fellow servants who owed him a hundred denarii, and seizing him, he began to choke him, saying, 'Pay what you owe.' ^{29}So his fellow servant fell down and pleaded with him, 'Have patience with me, and I will pay you.' ^{30}He refused and went and put him in prison until he should pay the debt. ^{31}When his fellow servants saw what had taken place, they were greatly distressed, and they went and reported to their master all that had taken place. ^{32}Then his master summoned him and said to him, 'You wicked servant! I forgave you all that debt because you pleaded with me. ^{33}And should not you have had mercy on your fellow servant, as I had mercy on you?' ^{34}And in anger his master delivered him to the jailers, until he should pay all his debt. ^{35}So also my heavenly Father will do to every one of you, if you do not forgive your brother from your heart."

First, because this is a parable, it is best read in its entirety before asking any questions. Consider the options for this:
- Choose one or two students to read the passage.
- Assign two or more verses per child. Have them stand up in front of the class in the order they will be reading. Stand behind the students to help with any difficult words as they read.
- Read it yourself to the students.

Each option has some distinct advantages. Whenever possible, it's preferable to have the students reading the text. However, for a long text such as this, there are some disadvantages:
- Slow or quiet readers may cause the listeners to lose focus.
- Constantly changing readers may be distracting and lose the flow of the story.
- There may be too many difficult words to possibly stumble over.
- Children may not be able to give the story the necessary/helpful tone.

In this case, with the text in our example, it might be advisable for the teacher to read it. But there are ways that you can encourage children to follow along in their Bibles. For example, in your lesson preparation, highlight several key words from the passage. Before reading the passage, explain that, as you read the text, you are going to stop at several points (your highlighted words), not saying the word that comes next. When you do this, they are to call out the next word. (This is another reason for using the same translation.)

Also, it may be helpful ahead of time to write out any unfamiliar key terms and their definitions on a whiteboard (e.g., 10,000 talents = an enormous amount of money; 100 denarii = a much smaller amount).

After the text has been read, it is important to lead the children through a systematic series of questions in order for them to understand the structure and meaning. Be sure to ask questions in a way that requires them to really look at the text so that they actually have to interact with it.

Examples of questions to ask from Matthew 18:23-35.
- *In this parable, we have three main characters or people. Who are they?*
- *Look at verse 26. What does the word "imploring" mean?*
- *According to the beginning of verse 27, why did the king forgive the servant? What specific word does the Bible use to describe the king's feeling toward this servant?*
- *Why is verse 28 surprising? How would you compare the debt of the first servant to the debt of the second servant?*
- *Look at verse 35. What is the warning in this verse? Who is the king in the story like—us, or God? Who are we to be like—the master or his servant? Do we sometimes treat others like the first servant treated his fellow servant? Ask yourself: Has there ever been a situation in which you have held a grudge against someone? Is there anyone you don't want to forgive? Is this pleasing to God? What would God have you to do?*
- As you can see, these questions are meant to take the students step-by-step through the passage. In a long passage, it is helpful to state specific verses you want the students to look at since it breaks up the text into smaller pieces that are easier to examine. Also, notice how the questions toward the end are aimed at the heart—each individual heart. The text is not just giving information; it is challenging their attitudes and actions.
- You might also want to ask the students if they can think of other Scripture verses that address the same theme. For example: *Can you think of other verses that talk about how we are to be forgiving* (e.g., the Lord's prayer, Ephesians 4:32)? This challenges them to recall prior information learned and see how it relates to other texts, emphasizing a unity in the Bible's message.

- **Demonstrate how to look for and make connections between important Old and New Testament concepts.** Children at this age become more curious about the relationship between the Old and New Testaments. When appropriate to the key themes of a lesson or Bible reading plan, point out these connections to highlight the unity of the biblical narrative. Here is a very simple example:

  John 1:29—The next day he saw Jesus coming toward him, and said, "Behold, the Lamb of God, who takes away the sin of the world!"

  Ask: *Why would John the Baptist describe Jesus in this way? In the Old Testament, what important role did lambs play in the forgiveness of sin? How did Jesus become like one of those lambs?*

  Another example:

  Matthew 1:21-23—"She will bear a son, and you shall call his name Jesus, for he will save his people from their sins." ^{22}All this took place to fulfill what the Lord had spoken by the prophet: ^{23}"Behold, the virgin shall conceive and bear a son, and they shall call his name Immanuel" (which means, God with us)

  Explain that the words spoken by the prophet refer to the words written by Isaiah about 700 years before Jesus was born. Connect the prophecy with its fulfillment. This example also serves to demonstrate the trustworthiness of Scripture.

- **Show them how to use some basic study helps such as a concordance, Bible dictionary, cross references, maps, etc.** These should not be too extensive or complex. It may simply involve showing them how to use the study helps included in their Bibles. A set of basic maps is also helpful to give the students a fundamental understanding of the location of important Bible places. Make sure to also include current maps so they understand, for example, that the kingdom of Babylon was in present-day Iraq.

- **Show the basic chronological order of the books of the Bible.** Children often assume that the order of the books of the Bible is also the chronological order. To correct this impression, a timeline showing the actual chronology of some of the major books is helpful.
- **Familiarize them with the basic classification of books:**
  - Law → Genesis, Exodus, Leviticus, Numbers, and Deuteronomy
  - Old Testament History → Joshua, Judges, Ruth, 1 Samuel, 2 Samuel, 1 Kings, 2 Kings, 1 Chronicles, 2 Chronicles, Ezra, Nehemiah, and Esther
  - Wisdom Literature → Job, Psalms, Proverbs, Ecclesiastes, and Song of Solomon
  - The Prophets → Isaiah, Jeremiah, Lamentations, Ezekiel, Daniel, Hosea, Joel, Amos, Obadiah, Jonah, Micah, Nahum, Habakkuk, Zephaniah, Haggai, Zechariah, and Malachi
  - Gospels → Matthew, Mark, Luke, and John
  - New Testament History → Acts
  - Epistles → Romans, 1 Corinthians, 2 Corinthians, Galatians, Ephesians, Philippians, Colossians, 1 Thessalonians, 2 Thessalonians, 1 Timothy, 2 Timothy, Titus, Philemon, Hebrews, James, 1 Peter, 2 Peter, 1 John, 2 John, 3 John, and Jude
  - Book of Revelation

Reading and Studying the Bible:
6th-8th Grade (Ages 12-14)

During this stage, students demonstrate a wide spectrum of both biblical literacy and spiritual desire. Some at this age are extremely proficient in studying the Scriptures and also exhibit a genuine and vibrant faith in Christ. Others show all the signs of intellectual knowledge of the Bible but show little evidence of spiritual life. Still others demonstrate genuine faith but struggle when interacting with the Scriptures. Finally, there are those students who seem bored out of their minds and you can barely coax them into bringing a Bible to class, let alone opening it up and doing serious study. While this presents unique challenges, it also should remind us of the necessity of addressing the whole child—mind, heart, and will—when we teach God's Word!

Main Goals
- Emphasize the inerrancy, authority, clarity, sufficiency, and necessity of Scripture.
- Train and equip them to more fully utilize inductive Bible study skills.
- Give a balanced approach to studying the Bible grounded upon these theological disciplines: Bible survey, biblical theology, systematic theology, moral instruction, and gospel.[32]
- Press in on the need to rightly respond to Scripture with the mind, heart, and will.
- Encourage the use of age-appropriate Bible studies for their personal use, including those that study one book of the Bible at a time.
- Expand upon teaching the fundamental doctrines of the Christian faith.

---
32 Please see the "Emphasize the whole counsel of God" section in Part 1 for the importance of this and a brief explanation of each discipline.

Content to Emphasize and Methods to Employ

- **Include specific teaching on the doctrine of Scripture.** This is an important age in which to highlight the doctrine of Scripture. There are many excellent resources, such as *Christian Beliefs: Twenty Basics Every Christian Should Know* by Wayne and Elliot Grudem; or *Bible Doctrine: Essential Teachings of the Christian Faith* by Wayne Grudem. Each provide chapters that are readily accessible for this age group. Furthermore, be sure of your own convictions concerning the Bible. If you take the Bible seriously, if you exhibit an unwavering confidence in what it says, if you demonstrate humble submission even to its hard truths, and if you express a heartfelt relationship with the Author of the Bible, the students will take notice.

- **When reading and studying the Bible, stress the importance of the objective meaning of the text.** In a culture that increasingly stresses relativist self-determination, it's important to continually stress that God's Word is objective, authoritative truth. The objective meaning is found by asking: *What does it say? What is the author's intent? What does God want us to understand? How must my thoughts, feelings, desires, and actions submit to this truth?*

- **Provide more formal training in inductive Bible study skills.**[33] Hopefully, at this point, they will have the basic Bible study tools at their disposal and are ready to move toward *self-discovery* when they read the Scriptures. This doesn't mean that they no longer need guidance, but when they open their Bibles, they should intuitively begin making observations and asking questions of the text. For example, they should be taught to...

    - Look for key words and phrases, repetitions, comparisons, transitions, etc.
    - Ask questions: Who, what, where, when, why, how?
    - Give a summary statement that accurately conveys the meaning of the text.

---

[33] I highly recommend Sally Michael's *The Inductive Bible Study Handbook*. It is a concise, excellent resource for both teacher and student alike (available at Truth78.org).

Here is an example from Colossians 1:16-20:

For by him all things were created, in heaven and on earth, visible and invisible, whether thrones or dominions or rulers or authorities—all things were created through him and for him. [17]And he is before all things, and in him all things hold together. [18]And he is the head of the body, the church. He is the beginning, the firstborn from the dead, that in everything he might be preeminent. [19]For in him all the fullness of God was pleased to dwell, [20]and through him to reconcile to himself all things, whether on earth or in heaven, making peace by the blood of his cross.

Students should be able to identify *who* is being spoken of here [Jesus] and then be asked questions such as,

How is Jesus being described in these verses? Why is this important? What things has He done? How did He accomplish this? What two words do you see repeated five times? What is the significance of this? How might you summarize these verses in one sentence? Why are these truths important for your own life? Do you honor Christ as "preeminent"? Are you reconciled to God through what Jesus has done for you on the cross?

- **Examine proper context by interpreting a passage in reference to the whole—what comes before and after, its historical and cultural setting, and how it relates to the overall message of the Bible.** For example:

Matthew 5:39—"But I say to you, Do not resist the one who is evil. But if anyone slaps you on the right cheek, turn to him the other also."

At first glance, the interpretation of this text seems very straightforward and clear. However, many people have misinterpreted it and used it justify absolute pacifism. This is an example as to why understanding *context* is critical. This verse is part of the Sermon on the Mount. It has a historical and cultural element that must be taken into account. The sermon as a whole addresses personal outward conduct and the motives of our heart. Furthermore, we must ask

the question: How does this particular verse relate to other verses that speak of responding to evil? Using a good Study Bible can be very helpful in understanding context and the meaning.
- **Encourage the use of underlining, highlighting, etc. while examining a text.**

  Here is an example from Psalm 19:7-9:

  The law of the LORD is perfect, reviving the soul; the testimony of the LORD is sure, making wise the simple; ⁸the precepts of the LORD are right, rejoicing the heart; the commandment of the LORD is pure, enlightening the eyes; ⁹the fear of the LORD is clean, enduring forever; the rules of the LORD are true, and righteous altogether.

  When having students make specific observations of a text, it may be helpful to print out the passage on a sheet of paper, and then have them mark the text. For example:
  - *Circle the terms that the psalmist uses in reference to God's Word.*
  - *Draw a rectangle around the terms that describe the qualities of God's Word.*
  - *Underline the type of effects that God's Word is able to produce.*

  This helps the students to better see the structure of the text as it highlights repetitions, comparisons, etc. These can then serve them in determining the message the author intended to convey.
- **Always address the heart and will when reading and studying a passage.** We cannot stress enough that biblical literacy has as its goal spiritual transformation—true repentance of sin, turning to Christ for salvation, loving Him as your greatest treasure, following Him in Spirit-empowered obedience, and living all of life for the glory of God! So, for example, when studying the passage from Psalm 19:7-8, press in on the heart by asking questions such as: *When you read these verses about God's Word, do they bring joy to your*

heart? Why or why not? Do you personally experience what the psalmist describes when you read the Bible? Can you give an example from your own life? Is there anything that may hinder you from experiencing delight in God's Word? Etc.

- **Give students time to study, discover, and respond.** As a parent or teacher, it can be very tempting to rush in and provide answers if we believe our children or students appear slow in responding. Be patient. Some children are slower than others in developing study skills. Others simply take more time to ponder and really come to grips with what the text is saying. Give gentle prompts if necessary, especially in a classroom setting where time is a greater factor, but be okay with momentary silence at times after asking questions.

- **Make clear connections between biblical truth and the students' own lives and experiences.** The Bible is not an old book that is out of touch with the modern world. It is, in fact, the only book that rightly makes sense of the modern world, and it is relevant to everything. The truths of Scripture also apply to everything the children/students personally experience—their fears, deepest longings, greatest joys, frustrations…and more. Help them make these connections as they read and study the Bible.

Here are two examples:

Psalm 33:10-11—The LORD brings the counsel of the nations to nothing; he frustrates the plans of the peoples. [11] *The counsel of the LORD stands forever, the plans of his heart to all generations.*

Questions to ask: *How do these verses speak to what is happening in our world today? Will evil rulers who make war have the final say? Will governments that allow and promote evil have the final say? Why not? Whose counsel will stand? Why can we be confident that God's will and plans will always win?*

Ephesians 4:29—Let no corrupting talk come out of your mouths, but only such as is good for building up, as fits the occasion, that it may give grace to those who hear.

Explain to your students that Paul wrote these words to Christians in Ephesus 2,000 years ago. But look at their relevance today in regard to how we talk on our phones, send text messages, and chat on Facebook. This verse doesn't simply tell us what not to do but offers instruction as to how to honor Christ and build up others in our speech.

- **Provide students with arguments for the reliability of the Bible (e.g., firsthand witnesses, historical and archeological evidence, manuscripts, etc.).**
- **Encourage the personal use of age-appropriate Bible studies at home.** Again, this may be done as a family during devotions. However, leading your child one-on-one through a book of the Bible would be very beneficial. Also, using a good study Bible[34] would provide numerous helps.
- **Make use of topical Bible studies/curricula that highlight the fundamental doctrines of the Christian faith.** For students in this stage of life, it's an ideal time to expand their understanding of the breadth and depth of the essential doctrines of the Christian faith. For example, provide biblical studies[35] that zero in on doctrines such as the character of God, creation, man, sin, Christ, salvation, the church, final judgment, etc.

---

[34] *The ESV Student Study Bible* (published by Crossway), while written with older students in mind, would prove very helpful if used along with a parent's guidance.

[35] See Truth78's Curriculum Scope and Sequence Explanation for suggested resources: Truth78.org/scope-sequence-explanation

Appendix

Key Verses Describing the Bible

- *Proverbs 30:5a—Every word of God proves true;*
- *John 17:17b—...your word is truth.*
- *Isaiah 40:8—The grass withers, the flower fades, but the word of our God will stand forever.*
- *Jeremiah 1:12b—..."I am watching over my word to perform it."*
- *Psalm 119:105—Your word is a lamp to my feet and a light to my path.*
- *Psalm 119:130—The unfolding of your words gives light; it imparts understanding to the simple.*
- *Hebrews 4:12—For the word of God is living and active, sharper than any two-edged sword, piercing to the division of soul and of spirit, of joints and of marrow, and discerning the thoughts and intentions of the heart.*
- *John 20:31—but these are written so that you may believe that Jesus is the Christ, the Son of God, and that by believing you may have life in his name.*
- *Romans 10:17—So faith comes from hearing, and hearing through the word of Christ.*
- *2 Timothy 3:16-17—All Scripture is breathed out by God and profitable for teaching, for reproof, for correction, and for training in righteousness, [17] that the man of God may be complete, equipped for every good work.*
- *Ephesians 6:16-17—In all circumstances take up the shield of faith, with which you can extinguish all the flaming darts of the evil one; [17] and take the helmet of salvation, and the sword of the Spirit, which is the word of God,*
- *Psalm 19:7-11—The law of the LORD is perfect, reviving the soul; the testimony of the LORD is sure, making wise the simple; [8] the precepts of the LORD are right, rejoicing the heart; the commandment of the LORD is pure, enlightening the eyes; [9] the fear of the LORD is clean, enduring forever;*

the rules of the LORD are true, and righteous altogether. ¹⁰*More to be desired are they than gold, even much fine gold; sweeter also than honey and drippings of the honeycomb.* ¹¹*Moreover, by them is your servant warned; in keeping them there is great reward.*

Bible and Memory Verse Activities

The following games should be viewed as a learning activity, and proper respect for the Bible should be encouraged.

Books of the Bible Games

There are a number of games that can be played to help children learn the books of the Bible. You may make up your own or use some of the following suggestions.

1. Write the name of each of the books of the Bible on a folded sheet of paper. String a clothesline across the front of the room. Hand the children these sheets as they come in, or hide the sheets around the room. The children then approach the clothesline and try to arrange the books of the Bible in order. Adults should be on hand to help the children look in the table of contents in their Bibles if necessary.

2. Split the class into two teams. At the signal, someone from each team can run up to the board and write the word "Genesis." He must then run back to his team and hand the marker or chalk to someone who is raising his hand. That person can then write "Exodus" under "Genesis." The game continues until all the books are listed. If a team gets stuck, someone may look at the table of contents, but the team then receives a one-person penalty. (They must wait while one person from the opposing team writes a book of the Bible on that team's list and hands the marker or chalk to another team member.) The team that finishes first wins the game.

3. For each child, make a set of slips of paper with a name of a book of the Bible on each slip. (These can be easily made by copying a list of the names and cutting them apart with a paper cutter.) Children must place the slips in order. When they have finished, they may help a friend. In the beginning, children may need to use the table of contents. Slips can be kept in an envelope and used periodically.

4. Next Card Please—This game works best if you have six or more children. Using a set of cards with the name of a book of the Bible on each card, deal out cards to every child. Have the children stand in a line a few feet away from a table. Explain that the object is to place all the cards in order on the table as quickly as possible. Use a stopwatch to determine how long it takes. As the children hold the cards so they can see them, start the game by asking who has Genesis, and have that child run to the table and place the card on the far left side. Then he will go back to where he stood on the line. The child who has Exodus runs up and places his card next. Continue until the children place all of the cards on the table in the correct order. Record how long it took. Then, set a goal to have kids beat their previous time and play again.

5. Write the names of the books of the Bible on the side of a cereal box using one box for each book of the Bible (so they can be stacked on top of each other, or lined up like books on a bookcase.) Using these books of the Bible blocks, play one of the following games:
    - **Order the Stack Game**—Divide your children into teams of two or three and have the teams take turns stacking the boxes in order. Give them a certain amount of time to stack. Mix up the boxes after each team takes a turn. The team that stacks the most boxes in the correct order wins.
    - **Books of the Bible Relay Race**—Divide your children into teams. Place the mixed up boxes and one team at one end of the room. Have the teams take turns picking up boxes, racing to the other end of the room, and placing them in order. Time how long it takes each team to complete the task. The team that completes it the fastest wins. Or you

can play using the whole class as one team. Time them to see how long it takes. Have them repeat the game to see if they can beat their time.

- **Which Book Is Missing?**—Pick five to 10 consecutive books of the Bible and display them in front of the class. Pick one child to remove one of the books (boxes) while the other children close their eyes or turn around. Have the children all turn around at the same time and see who can discover which book is missing first. The child who answers correctly first gets to take a turn and remove a book.

6. Print the name of each book of the Bible on a sheet of paper. (You may want to laminate the sheets.) Using the sheets, play one of the following games.
    - Put all of the pages on the floor and have the children put them in order.
    - Hand out the pages to individual children and have them line up in order.
    - Put the pages in order in a line on the floor (or have the children do it), and then have them walk beside the sheets reading the names aloud as they go down the line.
    - Put the pages all over the floor in order. Call out a book of the Bible and have the children find that page and go stand by it.
    - Similar activities can be invented to help children to learn other biblical information (e.g., the Ten Commandments).

Memory Verses

Spend time learning or reviewing memory verses. A variety of games can be played. (If you go directly to learning centers or small groups, small whiteboards can be purchased to use with these activities.)

1. Erase a Word—Write the memory verse on the board. Erase the verse a word at a time, each time asking the children to recite the verse.
2. Write each word of the memory verse on a slip of paper. Children must place the slips in the correct order.

3. Children line up or sit in a circle. Each child says a word (or phrase) of the verse, going from child to child.
4. Write the first letter of each word of the memory verse on the board. Children then try to write the verse.
5. Ping Pong—Children call out the first phrase of a verse; another child calls back the second phrase, and so forth. This can be played in pairs or in teams with the children facing each other in a line.
6. Children sit around a table. Someone writes the first word or phrase of a verse (or the reference) on a sheet of paper and passes it to the next person who writes the next word or phrase, and so forth until the verse is completed. The next person starts another verse, and so forth. By timing the children to see if they can "beat" their previous time, you can liven up the activity. Timing the activity may help you determine which verses and how many to include (e.g., see how many verses can they write in 10 minutes).
7. Have a "spelling bee" to review verses.
8. Make a word search using all the words in the verse.
9. Hot Potato—Have children sit on the floor in a circle. The first child says the first word of the verse and rolls a ball to anyone in the circle. The child receiving the ball says the second word of the verse and so on.
10. Line Up—Write each word of the verse on a separate slip of paper. Tape a slip of paper to the front of each child and have the children line up in verse order. (Variations: Play this as a team game or tape the slips onto the back of each child, have that child ask questions to find out which word is on his back, and then line up in verse order.)

Instructions for Sword Drills

Sword Drills are opportunities for you to have the children look up a verse in their own Bibles in a way that encourages participation and efficiency.

1. Start with the command, "Draw Swords." (You may want to explain that the term "sword" comes from the reference to the Word of God as a sword in Ephesians 6:17.) At the command to draw swords, children should hold their Bibles by the binding up in the air. No inserting fingers into the pages before the start of the drill.

2. State the reference clearly and slowly while you write it on the whiteboard.

3. Have the children repeat the reference.

4. Give the command, "Charge!" Children are free to start looking for the verse as soon as the command to charge is given.

5. When a child has found the verse—book, chapter, and verse completely—he may stand up. If there are students around him who are still looking for the verse, he should try to help them.

6. When all the children are standing, the teacher should call on one volunteer to read the verse. (Note: This should not always be the child who was standing first. If the first child standing is always the reader, children who are not as quick tend to grow discouraged and give up on participating.)

For children just learning to read, you may want to simplify Sword Drills greatly. Begin by having them just locate the book of the Bible you are reading from. As they become more familiar with the Bible and better readers, make it more complicated: Add the chapter number, then the verse number. It is important to remember that Sword Drills are not merely a *fun activity*. They are a way to help children become more familiar with the Word of God.

10 Essential Truths of the Gospel[36]

1. God is the sovereign Creator of all things. (Genesis 1:1; Psalm 24:1; Jeremiah 10:10a)

   What does this mean for you? God made you. You belong to God. God is your ruler.

2. God created people for His glory. (Psalm 86:11-12)

   What does this mean for you? God created you to know, trust, and love Him most of all.

3. God is holy and righteous. (Psalm 145:17a; Leviticus 19:2b; Romans 7:12)

   What does this mean for you? You must obey God's commands all the time.

4. Man is sinful. (Romans 3:20, 23)

   What does this mean for you? You have disobeyed God's commands. You are a sinner.

5. God is just and is right to punish sin. (Psalm 9:8; Ephesians 5:6b; Romans 6:23a)

   What does this mean for you? You deserve God's punishment of death and hell. You are helpless to save yourself.

6. God is merciful. He is kind to undeserving sinners. (Nehemiah 9:17b)

   What does this mean for you? You must depend on God's mercy in order to be saved.

---

[36] Taken from *The Greatest Treasure* by Jill Nelson, copyright © 2021, available from Truth78.org

7. God sent His holy and righteous Son into the world to save sinners. (John 1:14; John 3:17)

   What does this mean for you? God sent Jesus into the world to save you.

8. God put the punishment of sinners on Jesus so that His righteousness might be put on them. (Romans 5:8; 2 Corinthians 5:21)

   What does this mean for you? Jesus died on the cross to be punished in your place.

9. God offers the free gift of salvation to those who repent and believe in Jesus. (Romans 6:23; Mark 1:15)

   What does this mean for you? God tells you to believe in Jesus and repent of your sins and you will be saved.

10. Those who trust in Jesus will live to please Him and will receive the promise of eternal life. (John 14:15-16; 1 Peter 1:3b-4)

    What does this mean for you? If you are trusting in Jesus for your salvation, you must follow Him. Jesus has promised that when you die He will bring you to heaven to enjoy the greatest treasure of all...God! (Psalm 16:11)

Truth:78

Truth78 is a vision-oriented ministry for the next generations—that they may know, honor, and treasure God, setting their hope in Christ alone, so that they will live as faithful disciples for the glory of God.

Our mission is to inspire and equip the church and the home for the comprehensive discipleship of the next generation.

We are committed to developing resources and training that are God-centered, Bible-saturated, gospel-focused, Christ-exalting, Spirit-dependent, doctrinally grounded, and discipleship-oriented.

Resources and Training Materials

Truth78 offers the following categories of resources and training materials to equip the body of Christ and Christian parents:

Curriculum

We publish materials designed for formal Bible instruction. The scope and sequence of these materials reflects our commitment to teach children and youth the whole counsel of God over the course of their education. Materials include curricula for Sunday School, Midweek Bible programs, Backyard Bible Clubs or Vacation Bible School, and Intergenerational studies. Most of these materials can easily be adapted for use in Christian schools and education in the home.

Vision-Casting and Training

We offer a wide variety of booklets, video and audio seminars, articles, and other practical training resources that highlight and further expound our vision, mission, and values, as well as our educational philosophy and methodology. Many of these resources are freely distributed through our website. These items serve to assist ministry leaders, volunteers, and parents in implementing our vision and mission in their churches and homes.

Parenting and Family Discipleship

We have produced various materials and training resources designed to help parents disciple their children. These include booklets, video presentations, family devotionals, children's books, articles, and other recommended resources. Our curricula include take-home pages to help parents apply what is taught in the classroom to their child's daily experience in order to nurture faith.

Bible Memory

Our Fighter Verses™ Bible memory program encourages and equips the church, families, and individuals in the spiritual discipline of Bible memory. The 260 Fighter Verses passages have been uniquely selected for their ability to arm Christians to fight the good fight of faith by focusing on God's promises, His character and worth, killing sin, and hoping in God through the gospel. The 76 shorter Foundation Verses help toddlers and pre-readers lay a firm biblical foundation for life.

For more information on any of these resources and training materials, please contact us.

Truth78.org • info@Truth78.org
(877) 400-1414

GROWING IN THE WORD SERIES

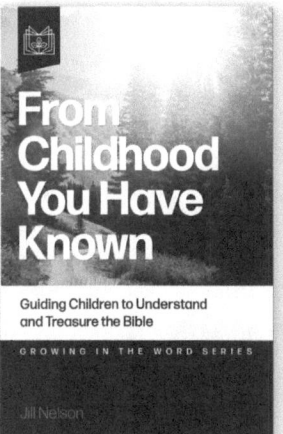
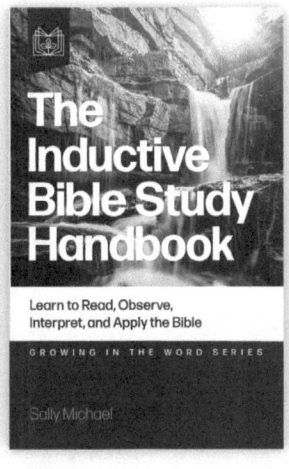
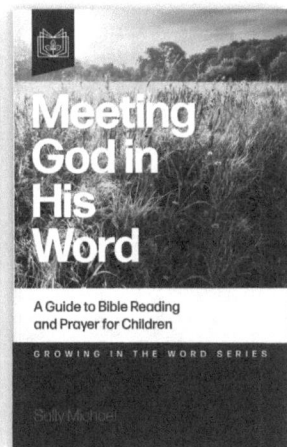

God has given us in the Bible a book like no other, and we have been given the great responsibility and privilege to pass its life-giving truth to the next generation. The Growing in the Word Series aims to inspire and equip the church and home to teach the next generation to read and study the Bible, pray for understanding and a right heart, and apply what they learn to their daily lives.

Resources in this series provide an introduction to the Bible, its message, and use; a reading plan; help with Bible memory and Scripture-focused prayer; age-appropriate training toward biblical literacy; and inductive Bible study tools to help children and youth learn to read, observe, interpret, and apply the Bible to their everyday lives.

Help the children and youth in your home and church come to know and love God's Word and, more importantly, the God who reveals Himself through His Word. Their very life and eternal joy depend upon it!

The following booklets are included in the Growing in the Word Series:

- **From Childhood You Have Known:**
  Guiding Children to Understand and Treasure the Bible
- **The Inductive Bible Study Handbook:**
  Learn to Read, Observe, Interpret, and Apply the Bible
- **Meeting God in His Word:**
  A Guide to Bible Reading and Prayer for Children

Family Discipleship Collection

Inspiration and practical help for teaching and discipling children

- A Father's Guide to Blessing His Children
- Big, Bold, Biblical Prayers for the Next Generation
- Children and the Worship Service
- Dedicated to the Lord: Five Parental Promises for the Faithful Discipleship of Children
- Discipleship through Doctrinal Teaching & Catechism
- Established in the Faith: A Discipleship Guide for Discerning and Affirming a Young Person's Faith
- Helping Children to Understand the Gospel
- Mothers: Disciplers of the Next Generations
- Praying for the Next Generation
- Utter Dependency on God, Through Prayer

Truth78.org/family-discipleship-collection

Zealous

Vision and framework for the discipleship of the next generation.

The next generation needs parents, teachers, and church leaders who are zealous for their discipleship. But where does zeal come from and what does it look like day today?

In *Zealous*, long-time pastor and Truth78 Executive Director, David Michael describes a fervor and diligence born out of a passion for God and His glory and presents seven commitments that provide a vision and framework for your discipleship of the next generation...so that they might set their hope in God (Psalm 78:1-8).

Truth78.org/zealous

A Guide to Growing Zeal for the Discipleship of the Next Generations

Apply the 7 commitments in your church and home

How can you make a vision for the discipleship of the next generations a reality for the children and youth growing up in your home and church? This guide offers practical application of the vision and framework presented in *Zealous*. Find next-step opportunities for each of the seven commitments for children's discipleship in this free PDF.

Truth78.org/grow-zeal

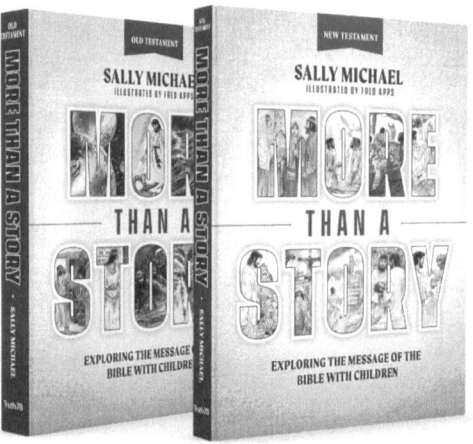

More Than a Story

Introduce children to a glorious God.

More Than a Story takes children (ages 6-12) on a chronological journey through the Bible with a God-centered, gospel-focused, discipleship-oriented, theologically grounded perspective.

Old Testament and New Testament volumes are available individually or as a bundle.

Truth78.org/more-than-a-story

Making HIM Known books

A series of books to teach children about the character and worth of God.

These illustrated family devotionals provide a way for the entire family to learn about our great God and His Word. Each chapter of these read-to and read-along books for elementary-age children ends with personal application and activities and is enhanced by full-color illustrations.

Each book is adapted from a Truth78 curriculum.

Truth78.org/making-him-known-series

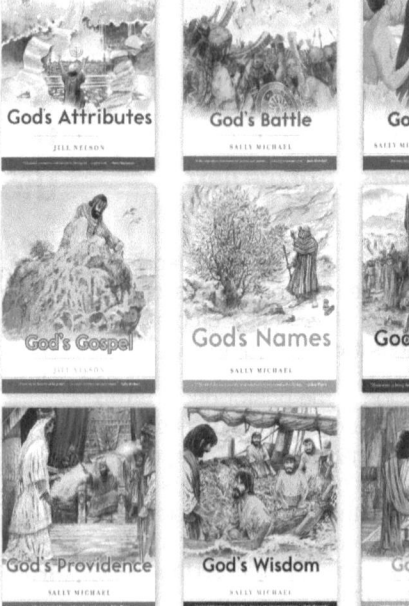

- **FighterVerses.com**—Provides an overview of the Fighter Verses program and its application for individual, family, and church use; includes weekly devotional blog, memory tools, and verse charts.

- **Fighter Verses App**—Portable encouragement with quizzes, songs, study, and review help. Includes additional Bible translations and multiple languages. Available from Apple, Google Play, and Amazon.

- *Hidden in My Heart*—A booklet to equip individual Christians, families, and whole churches to memorize Scripture.

- **Fighter Verses Studies**—Provide deeper study of the weekly Fighter Verses passages. Ideal for family and classroom use. Leader guides, participant guides, and coloring books for children available for verse sets one and two.

- **Fighter Verses Journal**—Includes a year's worth of memory verses with room for notes and written prayers. Available for sets one and two.

- **Foundation Verses Cards, Visuals, and Coloring Book**—Seventy-six short passages with illustrations to help toddlers and pre-readers lay a firm biblical foundation for life.

- **Memory Cards**—For those who prefer pre-printed paper cards.

FighterVerses.com

Good News of Great Joy products are simple Advent resources to help your family stop and reflect on the true meaning of Christmas, marvel at the providential events surrounding the birth of Jesus, and give thanks for God's provision of the One who has given us "the right to become children of God."

Good News of Great Joy resources include an Advent calendar, a children's book, and a coloring book.

These simple-to-use, reusable resources can become part of your family tradition as you remember together the birth of our Savior and the salvation He obtained for those who are trusting in Him.

Truth78.org/advent

Made in United States
Troutdale, OR
08/08/2024

21838482R20046